Young Naturalist
Field Guides

Tracks, Scats, and Signs

by Leslie Dendy
illustrations by Linda Garrow

Gareth Stevens Publishing
MILWAUKEE

For a free color catalog describing Gareth Stevens Publishing's list of high-quality books and multimedia programs, call 1-800-542-2595 (USA) or 1-800-461-9120 (Canada). Gareth Stevens Publishing's Fax: (414) 225-0377.

Library of Congress Cataloging-in-Publication Data

Dendy, Leslie A., 1946-
    Tracks, scats, and signs / by Leslie Dendy; illustrated by Linda Garrow.
      p. cm. — (Young naturalist field guides)
    "Based on the book, Tracks, scats and signs written by Leslie Dendy, first
published in the United States in 1995 by NorthWord Press, Inc., Minocqua,
Wisconsin"—T.p. verso.
    Includes bibliographical references and index.
    Summary: Describes how to find and identify footprints, droppings, nests,
feathers, fur, and other common clues left by sixteen wild animals as they
pursue their lives in woods, fields, and along ponds.
    ISBN 0-8368-2147-5 (lib. bdg.)
    1. Animal tracks—Juvenile literature. [1. Animal tracks. 2. Animals—
Habits and behavior.] I. Garrow, Linda, ill. II. Title. III. Series.
QL768.D46   1998
596—dc21   97-52129

This North American edition first published in 2000 by
Gareth Stevens Publishing
1555 North RiverCenter Drive, Suite 201
Milwaukee, Wisconsin 53212 USA

Based on the book, *Tracks, Scats and Signs*, written by Leslie Dendy, first published in the
United States in 1995 by NorthWord Press, Inc., Minocqua, Wisconsin. © 1995 by Leslie
Dendy. Illustrations by Linda Garrow. Book design by Lisa Moore. Additional end matter
© 2000 by Gareth Stevens, Inc.

Printed in Mexico

1 2 3 4 5 6 7 8 9 04 03 02 01 00

DEDICATION

To my father, the scientist, whose curiosity is still contagious. And to my mother, the artist, who saw beauty in every blossom and beaver.

ACKNOWLEDGMENTS

Much of the information in this book is based on the expert knowledge of wildlife scientists with lifetimes of tracking experience. The adult tracking books of Olaus J. Murie, Paul Rezendes, Chris Stall, Louise Richardson Forrest, and Preben Bang are highly recommended to anyone who gets hooked on tracking and wants to learn more.

I would also like to thank my husband and children for their help and encouragement on my own fact-finding field trips. Blair and Laura Swartz generously donated bear scat and squirrel nibblings from their yard.

The library staff at University of New Mexico-Los Alamos provided a never-ending stream of interlibrary loan materials and enthusiasm. And Barbara Harold at NorthWord Press helped me see the forest through all the trees.

CONTENTS

Tracks, Scats and Signs

Metric Conversion Table

1 inch = 2.54 centimeters
1 foot = .3048 meter
1 cup (dry) = 227 grams
1/2 cup (liquid) = 120 milliliters

INTRODUCTION

There are many wild animals in fields and forests and ponds. Some of them are easy to see, but a lot of them are not.

Wild animals leave clues everywhere they go. They dig underground tunnels. They make footprints in snow and mud. They chew plants along the way, and they leave droppings in their paths. They build nests. Their feathers and fur and dried skins fall off.

When you look for clues, examine the area carefully. Many clues blend in with the ground and the vegetation. Bring along a pencil and paper to draw what you see.

A magnifying glass is fun to bring along, too. Use the ruler on the back of this book to measure what you find. The more time you spend looking, the more clues you will discover.

TRACKS

Animal footprints are called tracks. It's easy to find tracks in the snow. You can also find them in soft or muddy places when you walk along a path or dirt road. Look at the mud along the edges of streams, rivers, and ponds. Look in the sand at the beach, too.

Hunt for tracks that show clear toe prints. Count the toes and look at their shapes. Look for tiny dots made by the animal's claws.

Be sure to notice the size of the tracks. Squirrels and raccoons both make tracks that look like little hands, but raccoon tracks are two or three times bigger.

SCATS

Dogs leave droppings on lawns, and people hurry to clean them up. Wild animal droppings are different. They tell the story of which animal came by and what it had eaten.

Scientists call these droppings "scat." Scat comes in many shapes and sizes. Most of the droppings do not have a bad odor.

Scats contain pieces of food that the animal could not digest. Rabbit droppings contain tiny pieces of twigs and leaves. Skunk scat is packed with insect bodies and wings. Fox scat may be full of mouse fur and bones one day, and blueberry or apple skins another day.

Look for scat near an animal's tracks or near its nest. You can use a stick to break it apart to see what is in it.

SIGNS

Wild animals leave many other clues about their busy lives besides tracks and scats. All the clues are called signs. A sign is anything you see that tells you where an animal has been and what it was doing. When an owl eats mice, moles, or voles, it digests the meat. Then it spits up a hard brown blob called a "pellet." It's full of fur and tiny bones and skulls.

Spiders let out liquid silk, which hardens into shiny threads. They use some threads as safety lines, like a rock climber's ropes. They also make webs to catch insects. Then they wrap some insects in tiny silk packages before they bite them.

A bird has thousands of feathers, and they fall off sometimes so new ones can grow. If you find a big pile of feathers, the bird was probably killed by a cat or a hawk. Or you can look for bird droppings on leaves.

Some wasps chew wood into tiny pieces to make paper. They build a tiny paper room for each baby, and wrap more paper around the outside.

These are just some of the signs you can look for to help identify which animals have been in the area.

BE SMART AND SAFE

Woods and other natural places are great fun, but they are wild. A tick or a snake could bite you. You could get sunburned or bump into poison ivy. Visit natural places only with an adult who knows how to avoid the dangers in the area.

Here are three rules that wildlife scientists use to stay safe:

1 Don't touch wild animals. They are normally shy and afraid of people. If a wild animal lets you get close, it is probably sick or injured. It could bite. Leave it alone and call the animal experts. Also, never touch baby animals or birds. Just because you do not see the parents nearby does not mean the babies are alone. Touching them may make the parents angry and dangerous.

2 Don't eat wild plants or berries, unless a plant expert tells you the items are harmless.

3 Don't touch animal nests or scats with your bare hands. They may contain bacteria, fleas, or other pests that could make you sick.

THE FOREST

For the animals that live in a forest, the trees and bushes are not just scenery. They are houses and food. Animals drill holes in the trunks or build nests in the branches. They gobble leaves, fruits, and nuts. They bite off the bark. They even eat the dead leaves and pine needles on the ground.

Look at the plants from top to bottom. You might see bear claw marks marching up a tree trunk. Down below, snails and slugs make their own slippery, slimy sidewalks across leaves and logs.

Leaves are like lettuce for caterpillars, grasshoppers, grubs, and slugs. Some of these creatures chew big holes or tiny tunnels. Others drink the sugary leaf juice and make the leaves shrivel. Many butterflies, moths, and bugs hide their tiny, beadlike eggs on the bottom of leaves. Then the hungry birds cannot find them — but you can when you know where to look!

RABBITS

Rabbits hop around
hunting for plants to eat.
And they hop in a hurry
to escape enemies like
owls and foxes.

Rabbit tracks are
especially easy to see in the
snow. When a rabbit hops,
its four feet land in a clump
shaped like a Y or a V.

Rabbit scats are hard balls,
the size of peas or marbles.
If you find a lot, the rabbit probably stopped
there to eat. Look for branches that were
bitten off with a diagonal cut.

A rabbit nest is like a bowl in the
ground. It may be hidden under a
bush. When a mother has babies,
she puts grass and some of her fur
inside the nest for them.

WOODPECKERS

What pecks all those holes in tree trunks? Woodpeckers, of course.

Hidden under the tree bark, many beetles and ants are chewing tunnels in the wood and laying their eggs. Woodpeckers can hear the insects chewing.

A woodpecker hammers its beak into the bark to make a hole. Its long tongue reaches through the tunnels and—zap!—grabs a snack.

Woodpeckers make bigger holes for nests.
The mother bird puts small wood chips in the hole, and
lays her eggs on them.

Many other animals borrow woodpecker holes
later. If you find one, it could have squirrels or owls or
raccoons inside.

SQUIRRELS

Squirrels leave their lunch leftovers on the ground. They drop empty acorns near oak trees. They chomp holes in hickory nuts and leave the shells behind. They also tear apart pine cones to eat the tasty seeds hidden inside.

You may also find a pile of little branches under a tree. Squirrels bite off small branches, so they can get the pine cones or tender buds at the end. They drop the rest of the branch to the ground.

Some squirrels make round nests as big as basketballs in the tree-tops. They build the nests with twigs, leaves, grass, or bark. Other squirrels live in old woodpecker holes.

Squirrel tracks look almost like doll hands. Look for them along a muddy road or in the snow from tree to tree.

PORCUPINES

A prickly porcupine can stab an enemy with its 30,000 quills. It doesn't need to run away fast. It waddles like a duck, and its tail drags on the ground. The quills make brush marks in the dust or snow.

When snow is deep, a porcupine just plows through, making a wavy ditch.

Porcupines climb trees to get tender twigs, buds, or acorns. They drop acorn shells and bitten-off branches under the tree. Some trees have huge bare spots where porcupines have pulled off the bark and eaten it.

Porcupine scats are shaped like peanuts or cashew nuts. They may be connected like a necklace.

DEER

Usually, you will only see deer as they leap away to hide. However, you can spot their paths and tracks through the forest.

A deer foot has two big toes with curved hooves. The toes may spread apart—or stay close together, making footprints like hearts. If the foot sinks into snow or mud, two more tiny toes may show.

Near their paths, deer leave behind piles of brown droppings that are shaped like grapes.

When a deer nibbles trees and shrubs, the chewed ends look rough. This is because a deer has no top front teeth. It rips a branch with its bottom teeth and lips. Deer also bite strips of bark off trees.

A deer "bed" is a mashed-down place in snow or grass, as big as a sled.

VISIT A ROTTEN LOG HOTEL

When a tree dies, it rots slowly. The wood gets softer. Animals dig and chew little "rooms" inside it, where they can stay safe and be warm in the winter. Even after they move out, you can see the signs they left behind.

It is fun to pick apart a rotten log or stump with a stick. Wear rubber gloves if you want to search through the log with your fingers. Make a list of the signs of life you find there. Be careful not to harm the little creatures.

1 First kick the log gently, to scare away any snakes that may be hiding inside. If the log is damp, you may see slime trails of snails or slugs on it.

2 Peel off a strip of loose bark. There could be a caterpillar or salamander underneath. You may see tiny tunnels, chewed by beetles and ants.

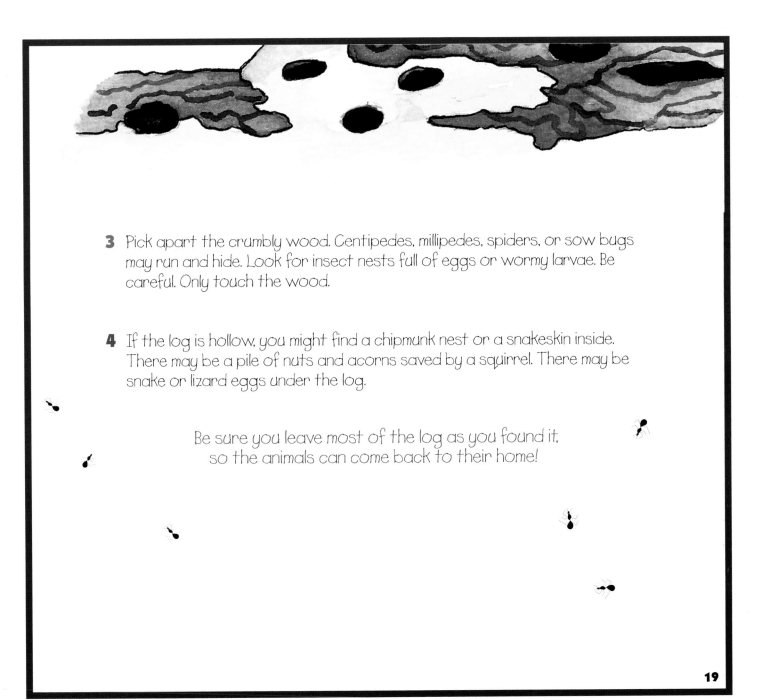

3 Pick apart the crumbly wood. Centipedes, millipedes, spiders, or sow bugs may run and hide. Look for insect nests full of eggs or wormy larvae. Be careful. Only touch the wood.

4 If the log is hollow, you might find a chipmunk nest or a snakeskin inside. There may be a pile of nuts and acorns saved by a squirrel. There may be snake or lizard eggs under the log.

Be sure you leave most of the log as you found it,
so the animals can come back to their home!

THE FIELD

Grasshoppers and butterflies are easy to find in a field, but many animals are hiding. Look for paths mashed down in the grass.

Hunt for little piles of dirt. These mounds could mark the "door" to the home of a dirt-digger, like a badger or a woodchuck.

Watch ants carrying food to their nest along tiny trails. The ants can smell their way. They make trails by dotting chemicals on the ground with their tail-ends.

Look closely at the plants. You may find a funnel-shaped spider web or a pile of grass pieces chewed by a mouse.

FOXES

Finding a fox is tricky business, but you can find fox tracks in a field or forest.

A fox paw print has four toes with claw marks. A fox often walks in a straight line. Its rear feet step in the same spots as its front feet. This makes a neat dotted line. If you see sloppier tracks wandering around, they probably were made by a dog.

A fox family often lives in a burrow that was dug by a woodchuck or badger. The "front door" hole is as wide as a soccer ball. When the foxes kick dirt out of the den, it makes a big pile on one side. You may find fox leftovers on the pile, such as feathers, bones, or mouse fur.

SKUNKS

Your nose knows when a skunk is near. A skunk can squirt stinky spray in an enemy's face. The smell can tell you where to look for more signs—if you dare!

You might find the skunk's sleeping place. It could be a hole in the ground or under a building.

Skunk scat is dark and chunky. Poke it with a stick. It may be full of bee wings or plant seeds or mouse fur. And you can guess what the skunk was eating.

Skunks have long claws for digging up mouse and bee nests in the ground. You may find the holes where a skunk dug. And you can see little claw dots in their footprints.

COYOTES

If coyotes live nearby, you may be wakened by their howling songs and barks in the middle of the night.

Coyotes run long distances in fields or forests, often along human trails. In the snow, the tracks go on and on. They often make a straight dotted line, like fox tracks. A coyote paw print is oval with four toes and two middle claw dots. A rounder print with spread-apart toes could be a dog's print.

Coyote scats are the size of fat hot dogs. Like fox droppings, they may be full of fruit in the summer, or mouse hairs and bones in other seasons.

23

SNAKES

A snake can slide between the blades of grass and sneak up on a frog. It can slither into a mouse tunnel.

How can an animal with no feet make tracks?

Under the smooth, scaly skin are many muscles. The muscles push the snake's body against every little stone or blade of grass.

The snake's whole body slithers forward and makes a curvy track.

This is tough on the snake's skin. But it can grow a new skin every few months, inside the old skin.

When it's ready to shed, the snake rubs its head on a rock or branch to tear the old skin. Then it crawls around. The old skin is peeled off, inside out. You might find it on the ground.

BADGERS

A badger can dig in the dirt faster than a human with a shovel. It tears numerous holes in the soil as it hunts for mice or prairie dogs that live underground.

A badger also digs tunnels and underground rooms for its own home. The "front door" hole on top is big.

Badger tracks have five toes and claw dots—like a skunk's but bigger. Badger scat may be full of fur and little bones.

WALK LIKE THE ANIMALS

Groups of tracks are great clues. Try making different track patterns yourself on a snowy field—or a vacant lot, golf course, or football field. Take along a tape measure.

STRIDE

The distance between footprints is called the "stride." Walk slowly across the snow. Measure the distance between your tracks, from one toe tip to the next. Now try running. Your stride changed a lot—it got longer.

Stride is a clue about how big an animal is. A muskrat's stride is about 4 or 5 inches. A moose's stride may be 3 feet or more.

HOPPING

You can hop with two feet. Rabbits, squirrels, and mice hop with four feet. The front feet land first. Then the back feet come down in front of the front feet. Put your hands down and try to hop that way.

How far can you hop? A mouse usually hops a few inches. A jackrabbit can hop 10 feet or more.

TIGHTROPE WALKING

Foxes and coyotes often walk in a very straight line. Walk across the snow as if you were walking on a tightrope. Keep your tracks in one line.

Foxes and coyotes do this with four feet. The back feet step right on top of the front foot tracks. Bend over and walk on your hands and feet. Try to copy the straight line of fox and coyote tracks.

THE POND

A pond or lake is a natural gathering place. Some animals live in the water. Others visit the pond to drink the water and eat the pond plants and animals.

Look at the mud along the shore for tracks. Some trails may lead away from the pond into a forest or field nearby.

Look at the plants near the shore. They may have been nibbled by ducks or insects. There may be bird nests hidden in the reeds. Dried skeletons of dragonflies may be stuck to the stems. You may see frog or fish eggs in the shallow water.

DUCKS

When a duck paddles across a pond, its webbed feet push the water like a diver's rubber flippers. When it walks on land, it waddles. You can see three straight toes in each footprint. You can often see the web of skin stretched between the toes.

A mother duck hides her nest in the reeds or grass at the edge of the pond. The nest is made of grass and some of her own soft down feathers. She lays her eggs there.

When the fluffy ducklings are strong enough to walk, they follow their mother to the water. Then you'll see big and little tracks together.

RACCOONS

The first raccoon sign you find may be garbage pulled out of a trash can. Raccoons often visit campgrounds and houses. They eat almost anything.

They eat plenty of pond food, too, and leave their own "trash" as clues. They drop crayfish claws and empty turtle shells. They make holes in the ground when they dig up turtle eggs. They tear up duck nests and scatter the empty eggshell halves.

Raccoons walk many miles around ponds and rivers, summer and winter. The tracks look like little hands. A raccoon's front feet work like hands. Its quick fingers can catch fish or frogs or crayfish under water.

MUSKRATS

When this fat rat runs around a pond, it makes hand-like footprints. Sometimes its skinny tail drags in the mud or snow, making curvy lines.

Muskrats pile up pond plants and sticks to make a lodge. Lodges are built out in a shallow pond or lake, or on the shore. Muskrats eat a lot of plants, and leave piles of plant stalks lying on the bank or on the water.

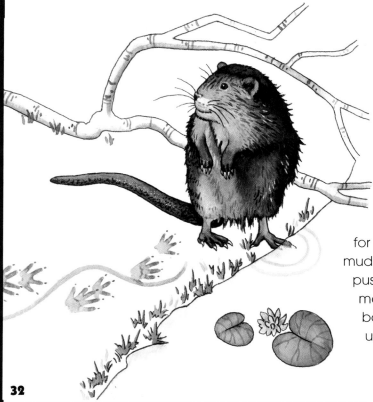

They munch clams and drop the clamshells. They leave peanut-size droppings on rocks or logs.

In the winter, muskrats make little huts for safe snacking. They collect plants and mud from the bottom of the pond. Next, they push it up through a hole in the ice, and make the roof for the hut. Then, they swim back under the ice to find food, and pop up into the hut to eat it.

TURTLES

If you see a straight stripe in the mud, with footprints on both sides, it's probably a turtle track. A turtle's stomach is close to the ground. If the shell drags on the ground, it makes a wide stripe. Sometimes only the tail drags, making a thin stripe.

In the summer a mother turtle lays her eggs in the ground. She digs a hole, lays the eggs inside, and covers them with dirt or sand. She may smooth the sand to hide the nest. Many raccoons, skunks, and bears can find it anyway, and eat the eggs. If you find a turtle nest, it's best to leave it alone.

33

FROGS

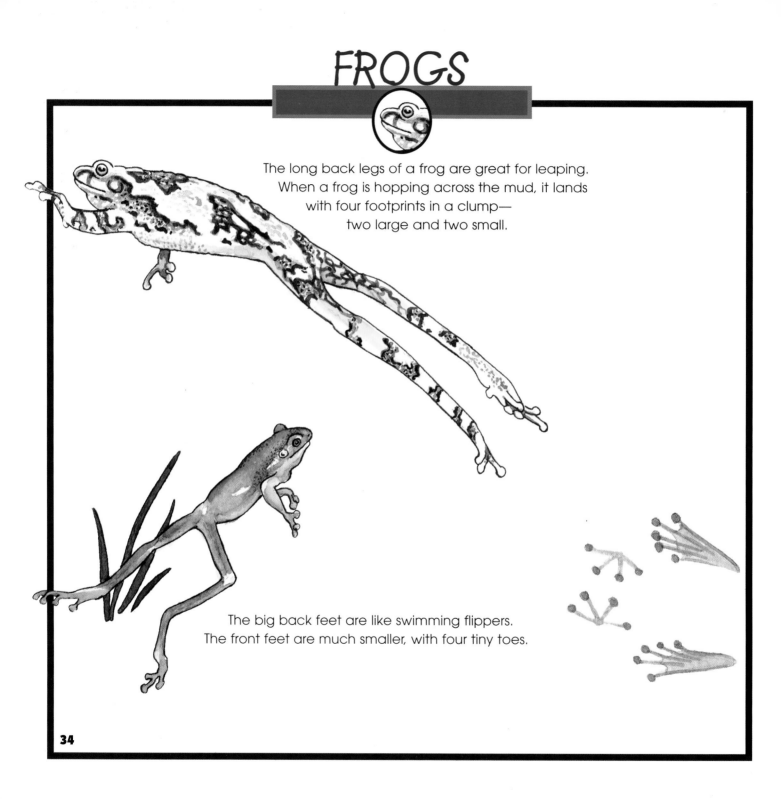

The long back legs of a frog are great for leaping.
When a frog is hopping across the mud, it lands
with four footprints in a clump—
two large and two small.

The big back feet are like swimming flippers.
The front feet are much smaller, with four tiny toes.

In the spring, a female frog lays eggs in the water at the edge of the pond. Each black-and-white egg, about the size of a peppercorn, is wrapped in a clear jelly coat.

You may find thousands of eggs in a gooey blob, clinging to the pond plants. Later on, tadpoles with tails hatch out of the eggs, and swim in the pond.

BEAVERS

Using its front teeth, a beaver can chop down a tree in three minutes! Pointy-top tree stumps tell you a beaver pond is nearby.

Beavers can make their own ponds by building a dam across a stream with logs and mud. You can see trails where the beavers dragged logs. A wide zigzag in the mud shows where a beaver's fat tail was dragging.

Beavers also pile up sticks and mud to make their lodge. The "doors" are hidden under water.

When a beaver eats, it twirls a branch in its paws like corn on the cob. It gobbles the twigs, leaves, and bark. Then it weaves the bare branch into the dam or lodge.

Beavers keep busy all winter. You can see log-drag trails in the snow, or a pile of branches sticking out of the icy pond.

After many years the beavers move away. If the old dam breaks, the water rushes out. Then a meadow grows where the pond was. But you can still see the dam and lodge poking through the grass.

MAKE TRACKS THAT LAST

Animal tracks can be collected and studied using this method. Fill the tracks with liquid plaster of paris. Let it harden, and then take the hard "casts" home. They look just like the bottoms of animal feet. This works best for tracks that were made in mud or soft dirt.

HERE IS WHAT YOU WILL NEED

- plaster of paris powder in a plastic tub or coffee can with a lid
- water
- measuring cups
- container to mix plaster in
- spoon
- pocketknife or table knife
- small box

HERE IS HOW TO MAKE THE PLASTER CASTS

1 Find some tracks first. Pick out two or three of the best ones.

2 Put 1/2 cup water in the mixing container.

3 Pour 1 cup plaster powder into the water.

4 Stir with the spoon until the lumps are gone. The plaster should be about as thick as pancake batter or applesauce.

5 QUICKLY pour the plaster into the tracks. Make sure it fills up all the toe holes and claw marks.

6 Let the plaster harden at least 20 to 40 minutes, until it feels as hard as a rock. Look around for more signs while you wait.

7 The casts are still fragile. Carefully cut the dirt around them with the knife, and lift them up gently.

8 Put the casts in the box to protect them on the way home. They will get harder after several hours. You can then rinse the dirt in the sink. A soft toothbrush helps.

For More Information

MORE BOOKS TO READ

The Amateur Naturalist: Explorations and Investigations. Charles Edmund Roth (Franklin Watts)
Eco-Journey series. Barbara J. Behm and Veronica Bonar (Gareth Stevens)
How to Be a Nature Detective. Millicent Selsam (Harper & Row)
The Kids' Wildlife Book. Williamson Kids Can!® series. Warner Shedd (Gareth Stevens)
Secrets of a Wildlife Watcher. Jim Arnosky (Lothrop, Lee & Shepard)

VIDEOS

A Science Walk With David Suzuki. (Beacon Films)
Tracking in the Desert. (Children's Television International)
Trail of the Buffalo. (Encyclopædia Britannica Educational Corporation)

WEB SITES

www.nwf.org/kids/
www.fws.gov/index.html

Some web sites stay current longer than others. For further web sites, use your search engines to locate the following topics: *ecology, footprints, tracks, wildlife habitat,* and *wildlife tracking.*

INDEX